Magic Words

J.A. Moretto

BookLeaf
Publishing

India | USA | UK

Presentation by *BookLeaf Publishing*

Web: www.bookleafpub.com

E-mail: info@bookleafpub.com

ISBN: 978-93-5744-949-6

First edition 2022

DEDICATION

To Aunt Nina and Aunt Roey who are always remembered and in my heart.

ACKNOWLEDGEMENT

A special thanks to all of those people who have ever taken the time to read anything I have written before, be it long or short. A special thank you goes to Rachel Druker, whom gifted me this opportunity.

PREFACE

Magic has always fascinated me. The idea that someone simply saying the correct phrase could make amazing thing happen stood with me ever since I was a child. As I read more and more and dabbled in writing, I soon realized that while it was impossible to make a car or large animal disappear, words still had amazing power. The power to heal or harm, the power to motivate or discourage, the power to completely change how someone sees reality: in short, magic.

The phrase "Magic Words" is a redundancy. All words are magical from the sweet whisperings of a loved one, to whatever you decided to call the person who cut you off in traffic this morning. It is my hope that the few poems (if they can be called that) transcribed here fill you with some sense of magic. Even if that magic is how someone with precious little talent can waste your time. That being said, I hope you enjoy at least one of these poems. Abracadabra, and happy reading.

Warning

They warned me I would lose myself if I
Kept my nose in a book and filled my head
With nonsense; or that life would pass me by
If I wasted it playing games or cards;
Because the real world was waiting and these
Trivial amusements were distractions.

In the end, they were right; I lost myself
But in the process I found so much more.
And what I found, and the joy it's given me
Are worth more than the real world
Could ever possibly hope to offer.

Quixote

When I was still a young old man,
They say I went insane.
They took away my lance and helm
And replaced them with a cane.

When foolish folly I pursued,
My life possessed some joy.
Now that it all has been dispelled.
Life just seems to annoy.

So once again I have chosen
To leave my house behind.
I will seek fortune's wild winds
To see what I shall find.

This time, however, I'm not plagued
With visions like before;
But I will travel once again
and be a knight once more.

Dulcinea does not exist,
Yet still she cheers me on.
No giants shall I fight this time;
Windmills, I'll charge upon.

Go tell Sancho, my faithful friend,
To ride fast if he can.
New adventures await us for
Quixote rides again.

Haiku

A simple Haiku
Can lead one to discover
The beauty of words.

Siren

My ears ring with the melody,
Heard since men sailed the sea,
Oh how I tried resisting,
Yet how it beckoned me.

I see all of the warning signs,
That prophesize my doom,
I hear the sweet song leading me,
Directly to my tomb.

The scuttled wrecks about the shore,
Like headstones do they lay,
Yet I glide across the water,
Without any delay.

Does Poseidon reward boldness,
And Aphrodite love?
Or do my prayers fall on deaf ears,
To anyone up above?

I have seen no sign from heaven,
No omen from on high,
We all know how this story ends,
One more sailor left to die.

But I'm not afraid of drowning,
I know I chose this part,
Either I'll sink beneath the ocean,
Or earn the siren's heart.

City

In the city, you're surrounded by the
People, going this way, that way, all ways;
never stopping, focusing on where they
need to be; they don't notice anyone.
You can blend in, you can hide, but you can't
Get them to stop and see that you are real.
To them, you are a ghost, a phantom, a
shade in between two worlds, a mirage
caused by a momentarily misplaced
ray of sunshine striking their eye just right.
Only in the city, surrounded by
people, can someone truly feel alone.

Insanity

"Insanity has its benefits," said
The man with the cane and top hat looking
At me from the chair I knew was empty.

Devils

Can you feel the heat as they rush towards you;
Smoke trailing behind them;
Watching and waiting as they approach
With pitchforks sharpened just for you?

You feel the heat, but it's too late
As the sky turns red and the infernal trumpets
blare
Announcing their victory, while the scores of
demons
Assembled to watch your torment cheer and jeer.

All you can do is hang your head
All you can do is accept your fate
And watch as they drink from the sacred cup
Knowing you can never get a taste.

Silent

There exists, I am sure, in some old, ancient
tongue
The word or phrase I need.

And once you hear, you'll know
How much I care for you.

But until I find it,
I must remain silent

Because I cannot risk losing you
Due to some errant slip of the tongue.

Drink

Drink with me friends, the day is here,
Drink while the sun's in the sky,
Celebrate another day,
But tomorrow we may die.

Drink with me friends as noon arrives,
Drink as you toil and try.
The day is long, but we are strong
But tomorrow we may die.

Drink with me friends as evening comes,
Drink be it bourbon or rye.
We toast to life and to love,
But tomorrow we may die.

Drink with me friends, as night rolls in,
Drink and let out a cry
For we survived another day,
But tomorrow we may die.

Spotlight

When I take my place, shine the light on me
I want to be the one to catch her eye,
The stage is set for everyone to see
The time has come, and now it's do or die.

I want her to hear my voice trembling
While I passionately confess my love.
And while it's to an actress I will sing,
It will be her that I am thinking of.

I know she will not care when I appear,
I truly doubt I cross her mind at all.
But she is the only one I hold dear,
And like a curtain, I've seen myself fall.

So make sure that you do your job tonight
And I will dream I'm wanted in her sight

Masquerade

Come see the masquerade, come see the show;
Disguise yourself and join the fun until
The sun comes up; see smiling faces happy
To see you here, for everyone's a friend
Tonight; but come the day you will receive
A different welcome; scowls replace the smiles,
And friends you found the night before have
gone.
But, the masquerade continues; for though
The night must end, the crowd still wears their
masks.

Dice

As I step up to the table, he shakes
The dice like gold, and that nice man in the
Red suit smiles as warm as ice and offers
Me the cubes, and says "Care to roll, my friend,"
In that singsong voice, that sounds exactly
Like nails on a chalkboard; and sends a chill
Down my spine that burns like a winter's snow.
"You risk it all, but you could win much more"

Remember

15

When called, I served; and I was loyal as
Could be; I never asked for any type
Of reward beyond recognition of
The many deeds I performed; However
Now, as I remain hidden in shadow,
I hope they'll remember all that I've done
When finally, they spit on my grave

Garden

Sometimes I feel like a weed in a garden
Waiting for someone to pluck me from the
ground.
Until I am discovered, I try to blend in.
Hoping no one who tends to the flowers sees
That I do not belong; because once they know,
They'll throw me out so I will not defile
Such a beautiful place by being useless.

Peace

To some I am gentle as a breeze,
To others, a gale force wind.
I am the soft glow of a candle
Finally flickering out.
I am the inferno which burns
Everything around me.
I am the peaceful shadow
That slowly creeps in the corner,
And the blinding light that you last see.

We have never met
Yet I have known you
Since you first drew breath.
When we meet, I cannot
Promise anything, except
That when at last you see me,
I will take you with me
In my arms, and, at long last,
You will know true peace.

Specter

This specter that haunts me can't be outrun
Nor can I stay hidden or avoid it,
But, I have learned, that with time and practice,
I can delay it from capturing me.
Evasion is the key; it will catch up,
And when it does, its icy chill will freeze
Me in my tracks; now, for just a moment.
Before it left me paralyzed for days
Until I slowly thawed and felt alive.

I know there's many people fighting
This specter; to them I say continue
Your Efforts, but know this: you can't beat
The specter completely, it will always
Be haunting and hunting; but you can keep
Away for as long as you can, and should
You find you're caught in those cold, glacial
hands,
Just brace yourself, until you're warm again

Time

The ticking of the clock, the grains falling
From an hourglass all remind me that
Time progresses; Yet I remain here still.
But there's still so much I want to do and
So many things I wish I did when I
Had the chance to do them; I look back
And ask myself "Why did I waste my time?"
Still, the fact that the clock ticks and grains fall
Tells me that I still have time; time to love,
Time to learn, and time to grow, and I have
Grown so much in what seems like such little
Time that just maybe, there is still a chance.

Hope

The light of a small candle can dispel
The darkest shadows; a mere whisper breaks
Surrounding silence; the gentlest breeze
Moves the somber stillness; and a distant
Star can illuminate the nighttime sky.
So long as a candle flickers, as long
As voices speak, until the last breeze blows,
And while a star still shines softly at night,
Rest assured, even when doubt surrounds you,
The smallest bit of hope can light your way.